ISBN 979-8-9913942-3-9

Published by Hidden Hand Press
www.hiddenhandbooks.com

HIDDEN HAND PRESS

# Death

# and

# the Insatiable

Mark A. Hill

# CONTENTS

About the Author

# Preface

*Death and the Insatiable* has been written over the last twenty years. I hope you enjoy my will to experiment with words, form, and ageing, which I try to perform with love and humour. The collection contains several different styles and a wide range of subjects. I'd like to thank all family and friends that see themselves here between the lines, and equally those of you who do not. I would like to think that there is a little bit of all of you in what I have written.

# HER DEPTH

He thought long and hard on her,

How she walked and

Moved with caution—

The way she loved, and roamed

The grating ocean.

He knew the colour of each

Of her dresses and her shoes,

The gravel depth of her eyes,

The way she crossed her arms,

The curve of each heel,

Her outer thigh.

She had caught him looking,

"I'm not put out," she had offered, then sighed.

1

On the shore, he raised his voice a little,

She wore the green dress and her skin cried.

"So, what I felt was more than beautiful?" ardent, earnest,

"That was why it was so cruel," she replied.

## STRYCHNINE

Strychnine poisoning may occur from the ingestion
of baits to be used on gophers, or

Coyotes;

It would be solemn, not in jest.


Some animals are immune to strychnine;

Crikey, just strike him! I hope he is not one of those.


There are species like fruit bats that have evolved a
resistance;

I'd have to check if he were a fruit bat. Can he bat?
Does he fruit?


Among domestic animals, dogs and cats are at risk;

Benji would have to be kept inside.

The first clinical signs of poisoning include anxiety and stiffness of the neck;

He'd always been a stiff-neck.


The convulsions flow with increased rapidity, severity, and duration;

These could be mapped on a graph; a chance to do maths.


I welcome asphyxia, a prolonged paralysis of the respiratory muscles;

He will breathe no more and I will slope home.

# THE CROWS AT MY LIVER

I am laid beside a green ladies' bicycle

While the crows perch and ponder,

Tick and consider. When I am not able to resist, they

Peck my peppered liver.


When they saw me on my bike

What were they thinking?

Wind in my eyes,

Why was I blinking?


Why is he not metalled-up in the wicked toy,

Like the others?

Why is he not bombing and swearing,

like his armoured brothers?

I was clipped by a lorry

Near my local roundabout,

Flew to the beach

Halfway into town about.


It wasn't anyone's fault,

like my calls to the past,

life will be elbowed

time will be cast.

# A Corpse on My Tiled Veranda

His passing

Would be in Pirri nineteen years before mine.


No pause,

I never saw him rest.


Open-shirted at his fall,

Driving sun his body baked and smoked.


You called

And told me that he was dead upon my roof.


They'd been married 40 years

And she never saw this coming

Although she had,

But the solace was of a blunter hew


Lay there amongst us,

And the ambulance would not take him away.


No hope,

They could do nothing and their time would be better spent.


What's that?

The sound of the neighbours' troubled dogs


His stories

Of my father-in-law and his refusal to pay up or conform.

You call again

and ask me how things might proceed.


Well, Italian tears

And there, honesty in howl.


I couldn't help

Hearing those lively clipped phrases he'd painted the day before.


We dragged him down the spiral staircase.

One rigor mortis fish leg blocked inside an eight-inch aluminium railing.


Formation of myosin—

The coagulation of the contents of the individual muscle fibres.

We trawled him up

And then down again.


His wife to recall their days together,

Took him away and insisted on sleeping with the
body.



The must—

A modal, an obligation or necessity.


People who work toward death

May consider retirement a chance to stop,


To pause,

But maybe it has all passed too quickly.

You got stuck in my stairs

And were then taken to the earth.

# Dropping a Tab of Keats After the Wedding

Blaze morning and my future is written,

My limbs are rum and thunder.

Though I held myself fall and gummed fine last night,

'Tis like I have wedded hemlock and coriander.


Without sordid trials of recrimination,

I will not slobber strained like Burton's child,

With my crumpet mind and memory stilted,

Consider what the breeze brings, will it harbour life.


Sure, I'm happy when you're happy.

Especially if we're plotting to go off on one, do a runner

Or carping 'bout the nite before,

Off to bawl out the copper sky in Old Havana.


I flee now to the forest with my blushful bride,

Let's drink *Ichnusa* and toss the bottles spare,

With burlap bubbles at the brim of bags,

Boredom at tomorrow's barking signs, standard fare.


When I write as an old man, I will cry in dirge and trolling,

When I wrote as a young man I scribed of love in rhyme.

But now in the middle lines, what to write on not to seem

Too gay, or grained before my time?


Today we sit and reach for each other's monotone.

My first palsy shakes from wavering limbs forestall
the sentry.

The sullen grey hair, where youth is dead and tooling
bleeds,

Where love is blood lines dropped in milk; no entry.


I called you sweet names all too often,

Drew you to the ground beneath my gargoyle teeth,

A hanging will to ecstasy in gaudy taunts,

Taken to dampened sod with barley breath.


When nothing was aged, all was straggled, thrown,

you stood in fields of corn—our love was tears on
vine.

Lay open your fettered form, let fly

Those simple seeds in minor chords and chamomile.


Falsehood is a word that whores like a bell.

Embrace the future, mend the heart around,

Or form the lines as the gentle Sycamore

helicopters that miller ably to the ground.

## DASHED HIM

"I'm hot now," he said and placed

the sheet on the

mattress.


She tucked it in

looking for

order,

then took a case

and covered one

pillow.


He was troubled,

but reciprocated.


"I'm hot now," he said

Then hummed tunelessly
to himself.

When he lifted the bed,
she took a thinner duvet that
would provide less
heat.

"I'm hot now," he said
And in some way,
his woman wasn't there.
He went to the bedside table,
got out his ill-matched socks,
looked over at her and
shot a missive.

After all these years,

he got the

shit on it;

she hadn't loved him ever.


He walked through the door,

opened the mosquito net,

stepped over to the balcony edge,

tipped gently

and dashed himself—

pepper

on the pavement

below.


The next year, she had a new man,

with a full moustache

and arms of willow.

He ate well

and earned well,

he was good to her in bed,

which is often what is

required.

# THE SALAD BOWL

We motioned to the kitchen and she took the salad deliberately

From the picnic basket.

Lettuce, cucumber, home grown beef tomatoes and,

Without use of a board,

Cut them leisurely into a wooden bowl.


She added three spoons of olive oil and seasoned generously,

Her figure made me gape.

I remember she had on her glasses.

She was scholarly, but at the same time tantalising, voluptuous, irresistible.

Her form could not go unanswered.

I lit a cigarette and tried to get a grip;

I wasn't good at getting a grip.

It's now or never said my brain

(I use the word brain in the broadest possible sense).

I fell to my knees and flung my arms around her Latina waist,

Attempted to burrow my head between her legs,

To return from whence I had come.


"I love you," I cried; I need you!"

I had pondered more class, more roundabout,

But sometimes the *now* doesn't keep up with the plan.


I just let her have my sophistry both barrels.

She turned her hips and tried to escape my clammy grasp.

I clung on to her skirts like a baby panther.

She raised the salad bowl and brought it crashing down upon my head.

I was at once a dizzy inundation of salad, mayonnaise, olive oil—

Addressed metaphor of my attempts to see her unladen.

"You're a fool," she cried, "a lunatic,"

But I saw no sense

And pawed at her frantically.

We were caught in meaningless combat,

A shell of a man and a beautiful woman.

She crawled away from me and into the bedroom,

And I went away later that same afternoon.

## SWAN VESTA

She was my second love prescribed.

Back then she came by cycle light,

Fine one furtive evening I tied

Her up, falling worked a lullaby.


I matched her close in callow swallow

Pried her long legs open, willow hollow,

With ether held her for twenty seconds,

Swooning till her falling beckoned.


A child amongst beeches, her spinning corpse

Did caress the lofty branches,

Vain called the sentinel in wing

As I stroked, then lit up with sulphur matches.

# ADJECTIVES

Cezanne altered our perception of size

until the small became all we saw.


Updike painted trees,

drew ladies' knees,

and discriminated in the use of adjectives.


Hemingway never used them,

but let his characters loom large

to talk and act their way through tasks.


True to the fenced coppice of our infancy,

they called the now

and by definition moderated our style

at the roulette wheeled dances

before black-berried hedgerows.


We wore our adjectives proudly like badges on
school blazers

and poured lovely custard utterances

into the straw dullard of our own growing up.

## MILANESI AT THE DEAD SEA

In front of bibled Palestine,

Looking at a little bit of geography and a whole lot of history and religion,

I'm moved to write something later.


"Come in it's..."

"It looks cold..."

"It's not, come in..."

"It looks really cold..."

"Come in *dai*..."

"I don't want to."

PUTS TOE IN WATER AND MAKES SHARP EXCLAMATION OF RUIN.

HUBBUB FROM THE WINGS.


"It's cold..."

"It's not cold *dai*..."

"It feels cold..."

"Come on, just for a minute or so; it's not as cold as it feels..."

"It's cold..."

"*Dai*..."


Ad infinitum—

My son and I cover ourselves in mud.


Just *dai*, please.

# MAGPIE QUESTIONS IN BRYNMILL PARK, SWANSEA

(No ideas but in magpies)


I ignore the one-two because

that's what I do, and

calculate the likelihood that

I will see you.


Jenny, Mike and Tommy

were three for a girl,

but were in fact one boy, one Boyd and one girl.


What is silver now,

if I see six,

a 10p, a 20p or 50p?

Would a seven bring

just a one-pound coin?

A pittance today,

with inflation and

the money supply call.


How might a story be a story

if it's never to be told?


Is it wrong that I should determine my day

by your number in the park

and then go to the

university to teach young

life about the value of

critical thinking?

Is there true valour or love in anything?

Why am I left here,

looking for the second magpie, whilst

longing for my childhood friend?

# SWANNING AROUND

Every morning I wrestle with my coloured sandwich
box

and perform a feint liquid rinsing of docile dishes.

I bow before this sink and scrape at chipped cups
and saucers—

the bold brillo pad choice to be made, cucumber
wishes.


I can hear your breathing through my phone in
ethered silence

like I can hear drip water cisterns in this collared
strain.

I am sick with always wanting you and knowing that
you

will never, in a swan of summers, yield fire to my
rain.

# THE GOLDEN GATE BRIDGE

You climbed out onto the girded Golden Gate
Bridge,

unapologetically high above the city,

the wrong quay side of a talky afternoon.


All drunk out with beer and clam chowder,

workers waved and gesticulated,

and I just sat there dumb; unresponsive

for four long minutes.


As your shirt sleeves danced,

there was something hulkishly raw about

your heron movements,

like there was some originality

in oyster, sea bream and rosehip,

like show jumping or cooking programmes

might bring either daytime TV, or what you called

*all of this* to a logical

conclusion.


On catching one outside glimpse of yourself

seeing your movements for what they were,

you paused, a little more afraid,

and caught a hold of the railing.


By this time, I was moving toward you

my arms outstretched to make a save,

you straddled the balustrade and

came landside.

I placed a jacket

over your shoulders

and tried to turn your head downwind to

port comfort for your jagged thoughts.


Carefully, I drove you home to an empty tenement
house

that held no records

and no player.

## INCOMERS

Immigrant - one who immigrates, from the Latin:
*immigrantem*


Who are you that knocks *chack* home in inked hue?

Who are you that would come in?

Who are you that colours my landscape?

I was not expecting you.


Incomers swim *chack* home

like unfettered crows

crashing to the water,

through the cobalt skies.

A shower of energy

with gum Arabic feet

to the edge of what you would call your own.

The shellac incomers call chack home.

"You enslaved my people,"

"Why so harsh?" you reply.


Incomers bounce like

drum percussion *chack* home

whirr the locals to concussion.

Transit may open lives to opportunity

while our continent's follied decadence slurs in
white collusion *chack* home,

in the car parks *chack* home.

Drivers err and cherry blossom falls *chack* home,

and crows' feet run *chack* home

*chack* home *chack* home.

# I Shall Never Be Light

You offer lines in an indigo yawn of inconstancy
        ow of in di
    nb              fe
   ai               re
ar                      nce


                    t
            h
          g
          i
But if I were l in your bidding,


                        t,
                    h
                  g
                  i
And I shall never be l,
It would only be for fear of the prize
Being greater than my heart,
Straighter and stronger than I s


                            t
                            a
                            n
                            d.
b 4 u...

37

# CAGLIARI, ITALY

The fisherman of Cagliari who strides from bar to bar is brave as a lemon tree,

Smites like an axe,

He plucks a flower from an almond tree

And hands it to his fiancée.


Whereas, everything might be its own opposite

When we strike poses and airs,

Politics wins friends, conjures enemies,

The pacing fisherman dares.


He salutes those who stir early to bake bread

Those who resist to dawn to toss Bacchus' coins on wine.

The tattooed trend is fish and be brave,

In old age, he will shelter, toe the line.

The English teacher strikes a gait in Piazza Savoia

And seldom errs from her plastic folder.

Her phone rings a Latin buzz

And she peers into it searching cold for the real caller.


The Marketing managers want to use the fisherman to net the disencrusted,

Those without bread.

They sought him in Castello cussed

With a jaw like metal, a head like lead.


Makeover came and went for him,

Women wept over him

And made him into a cinema idol.

His eyes bacterial, his visage viral.

Sitting at my bar watching this unfold,

Yearning for a steady hold.

How cultured is an Italian nose?

Dissimilar to the English rose.

# What's in a lick?

Pocket your tongue in your mouth, then release it quickly.

You have produced a lick.

Dental licks are those you practise

before your dentist after a visit,

using the tongue and the teeth to create an air pocket.

Native English speakers make these licks after expressing

disappointment (tut-tut).

If you are disappointed by your dentist, change dentist.

Lateral chick licks are the sounds generated from chicks' lips

during a chick flick. The mouth is opened

to create a space for the exit of the sound.

The click moves along the side of the tongue—

The male of the species has been warned.


Alveolar licks are performed using the palate ridge and the tongue

to create contact between articulators.

This is the sound of a trotting horse.

It can be used on long walks, bike rides and school outings

to entertain errant children.

## An Image of the Daughter

when the artist

offers


shelter from the eye, rain

falls, time


wraps the daughter up

in tempera


within this imposing

portrait.


centuries pass to sully foul over her

tender prime and

break her joyous

frame, yet she


has become the image

that is


gazed upon inside this country

home.

# BEAUTY MUST REPEAT

Each one of us breathes a life

created in a moment of beauty.

Mute The Larkin, and

in my wordy issue seek solution—

Procreation is increase not dilution.


Invest yourself—

make husband of your seed.

Do not bring famine where food is plenty,

fill the vase of life with bloom.

Leave your lover never empty.


Do not pause a moment to consider

the boys' pre-conceptions and the other lovers.

Never stall the finishing

accept all the bug eye offers.


Finger hard on the soft pork belly

of what is out there; living means

pawing dampness tenderly

meeting loving ends.


Feed on what could be struck or strikes you

what you swipe, not with AMEX, but with your ID,

your trace, your content,

which will be stowed away in your peerless progeny.

## Pasticceria Italiana

I walked into the pasticceria

and told the waitress that she had

made a rather poor show

and caused me none untoward

embarrassment.


She asked what I meant by this and I

told her that I had recommended this location to my wife,

but the doughnut they had sold her

had been undercooked on the inside.


She replied that it had probably been,

"short, rotund and ill-formed."

Only in Italian, the subject pronoun is omitted,

so I presumed she was describing my wife.


I responded that I was not aware that she had met my wife.


She said, "No, no, no, I meant the doughnut."

# Chutnification

As an introduction to the joy of the word
chutnification,

you ask me what is required.


Apples, raisins, fish, vinegar, spices,

a throated pinch of jaggery powder, love.


Daily visits from *bhaji* women with their coloured
*saris* raked

up and held on the outside of their thighs,


Cucumbers and yogurt, aubergines and mint,

but also my coldest blue eyes,


Which are undeceived by the superficial,

drawn like art, yet undeterred by your caprices.

Eyes which can see the flavours within the hearts of green tomatoes.

I supervise these legendary recipes; I know what goes into the pots.


Through my vision, my love, and the powered essence of mixing,

I give you my chutney in three small jars.


When you have the courage to taste it,

you must tell me what it does to your mouth.

# HER QUININE IN RIBBONS

She is braced, dresses thrown up, sprayed like paint, auburn

cast up on my canvas; she will ever be on me.


She is real as the sieve, even as the calendar, bray bray,

spoken for, she turns around and is the sloping bay she stands before.


I look back and nurse my aching fall as I run from her coast.

She is quinine and blousy, never trivial, taken from an honest man.


She waits for him and smites at me solemnly for what has come

from twixt mossy bible legs; I hauled songs to her
gerund sleep.


A horse's rest stop—a place to pause and sip bitter.
She is the render

I hold dear to my pillow when I cling to orphaned
slumber.


She is baritone when I take her by the beach

and tip my fine moustache to mop her ashen skin.


Her children watch as I play on her proud spread
limbs,

and toss a flat pebble long and true towards bottles
unannounced.


Piles of salty fish slop landward and a boat chokes

and pushes with the tide men as they roll home; one
is hers.

She gazes out to sea, mullet forms twist in their nets; her face flushed with what?

I give him back her heart that he might return and probe.


To my mind, he barbs her in an ice cream intermission,

her garter will fall, my flapping mouth wrought with altercation.


This will be the last time she is wrapped around me, an orange ribbon in her hair.

Answering the call of her protector, she is so naked and slovenly tall.


I slip away through the hills, a thief who has taken what he ought not have.

Her loyalty is studied admiralty, an afterthought.

Tomorrow there will be nothing left of us, slammed shut in the tomb,

blessed by a kissed intervention and trowelled deftly in bedded loam.

# 4-4-2

If those who watched football just

                            stopped

                            full

to see the beauty of a line

                            break,

                            corrupt

the sheer audacity, timing
of metre and rhyming,

what would they want to

                            become?

Or would they still will to

                            interrupt,

                            or raise their

cobalt arms

looking for an

offside?

# THE DRESSED WAR

A.

As cocked Roman numerals were not available.

B.

But even if they had been, it was unlikely that they would have revolved fine.

C.

Jack-in-a-box and Jack o' Lantern, Cola battle lines in crossword clues.

D.

Day, amphibious landings and airborne assaults.

E.

Emerging from the Normandy water, a vision, ever won—three teeth.

F.

Fraternal, inside or lateral, he fought on for valour and no one told him why.

G.

Growling to the fall, knife felled, sticked good,
whirled in sanguine colours.

H.

A soldier wounded in a car accident, juxtaposed,
maybe ginger Harry?

I.

At the lights by a circus truck, listening broiled.

J.

Up telescope in the sea of war, eyes fixed to win the
battle.

K.

The king pins his medal anyway.

L.

Leaders look on like limestone, pretending to be
scientists, then mime the future.

M.

Long and huffed by cenotaphs and deals brokered,
Bond watching.

N.

Never enough, nitrogen elbows on tables holding papers, no napkins at dinner.

O.

A pause, a moment of stoppington, or loss.

P.

Perplexed, we try to find the cause, the purpose to the prince or princess.

Q.

Where we stand, with products laden.

R.

The sorry scraping of the barbecue grill, the dentist's calling.

S.

S class submarines had ten internal bulkheads.

T.

For Chinese mouths.

U.

Boats to be tracked.

V.

Vodka with their main meal, a norm.

W.

Because we want to see what goes on under their cerulean water.

X.

The military exit, looking at the past and a chalky trumpeted withdrawal.

Y.

Not my retreat, what we always ask and fumble upon, the how and what will follow.

Z.

The zone we long to defend, the dressed war we fold down and hold around ourselves.

## Orchidaceae

If you should stay soldiers' arms

and solder them ashore solemn as their toil

as your long stamens sway nimbly

well-meaning in your artful graft, then strife

might end and pennies would reign fine change

upon the aged bedding of our lives.


But as a flower, your will to change all of this

is null and your ambition less—

the seed that you spring from

does not ponder wickedness.


You are a single orchid

seemingly most chaste, yet

you remain fertile for long periods.

A platform for pollinators

in racemose inflorescence,

canopied in a Mozambique forest,

where Darwin may have

spoken lessons.


Your seeds are microscopic yet numerous

like my night sleep jolts,

my ever so movements to the sunrise

that warn partners that my breathing is still real,

I have torn these words for years and eyes.

The drawn core of your labellum,

whored in odour, shape and colour

to mimic the receptive female,

calls my male insectry to honour.

Pollination will occur as I shake stale

and note you down, yet stay your stalled valour.


A weighty whole of mine will pass.

I am an intruder who strokes his shutting still

when chancing upon an orchid

framed beside a chosen path.

## ALL MY FRIENDS

All my political half friends, the chosen ones, the
*chinkers*, are in prison now—

those that had the stuff,

the owners.

And how did that come about?

I don't live in Russia or in books;

I live here in the modern.


The machinations

the road deals, guilty by association or the lack of
will to say no,

maybe they'll be released in June.

I know they have fine lawyers,

mine is Dickens' child and drawn in Lincoln green.

We will spend shedloads of money for the arguments
and such.

Williams' chickens peck,

Rothko offers lines,

Eminem sprays and splays like Pollock,

And we all look on.


We don't speak on the cell phone anymore,

only in person

with

lovely lent pauses,

the will to err

and fretful eupnea

blown off into the sky and wild strewn as the
mentally ill

or those who contend no more.

It all seemed easier at school—

they made it feel

like we were moving forward.

# ANASTASIA

I begged court that we would stop not being
together, and

She told me that I must stop trying too hard to
bring her softly to my ends.


I told her that in the next life we would be married,

She told me that this would likely be the case, but in
this time I should respect form.


When the words failed me, my gestures became
overbearing and fevered,

*This is your way* she indicated, *and this is mine*; a long
division.


I leant onto her stormed lips, rubbed low and
bellowed air—a genie caller.

She warned me to be tender and moved away
feigning indifference.

In moving she parted the air, I stayed in Sweeney's
room,

I am still sitting there, her indifference folded
tightly to my chest.

# Italian Phonology

"In addition to monophthongs,"
She told me.


"Italian has diphthongs,"
I listened true and fell straight into her syrupy eyes.


"These are simple phonemic and phonetic
combinations of other vowels,"
Wavy sounds, I thought, the wobblers.


"Like illnesses, some are quite common, while
others are rarer
and some never occur at all."
I was glad of that;
some never occurred at all.

"No diphthongs are considered to have

unique phonemic status because their

parts do not behave

differently than they would in

isolation."

Well that's clear, I would repeat that verbatim; not paraphrase.


"Like politicians in bellyful mid-manoeuvre, football coaches and singing stars,

we distinguish between falling and rising diphthongs. However,

since rising diphthongs are composed of one demi-consonant sound

like /j/ or /w/ and then another vowel sound,

they are not technically diphthongs."


My thesis would read,

Luciano Canepar criticised the practice of calling
them diphthongs.

He got really cross about it, he scattered books and
sprinkled words

Like icing on a cake.


And my lovely professor asked me to give more
rigour to my thoughts,

lend more depth to my critical thinking and return
the following fall.

## WEEDS IN TENURE

That weeds in tenure might be held

In torrid land the scorched lawn.

Birds hop, hoe rides, the weather scorns

So slowly grown, seeds newly strewn.


You withering weeds that meet

Your life blood in cussed land

Lying long ignored in the heat

Unearthed vagaries in sand.


What worlds now steal over you

Embrace my warm chemical spray.

Your living nature's yawn

The reaper on a sunny day.

As you die I shall not smile

Though the springtime now is mine

We lovers, in the fading light,

Would honour summertime.

# CHAUCER'S LONDON MERCERS

A ship set out from Temese

In search of foreign duty free,


Men were blown back to the border of Kent

Out to sea and homeward sent.


When asked for water and eggs

Good wyf bent her stoic head,


Judging by his language and his foreign stenc

She answered she could speak no *Frenshe*.


And the merchant was at a loss

Because he could speak no *Frenshe* also.

When he asked for eyren

She understood him well.

## ALL ALONG THE GALLERY

Today

the sun reflected

off the road

into the gallery

at an angle.


People barricaded themselves inside

tenured with the A/C.


All that was left

was *sa basca*

the warm clay lung wrap

of old rolled tobacco.

I folded myself

inside the oven

like an unpegged towel

then walked over

towards you

and called your name.


I held that you would recognize me

and as the heat wafted me along,

damp sweat inching up my boxers,

You turned and raised your right arm

like an airport courier

or a puppet

with only one string

attached.

# AT THE CRUCIBLE

You can stride around the table,

manipulate the rests and cues, scratch at the light
blue chalk,

as often as you choose.


There are no Arthur Miller references here.

This is not a central hue in the USA vulture,

although snooker was once essential UK TV culture.


You can take a rest from the baulk end,

you can miss an easy red,

then do penance with water.


You can even shake hands with the temptress
anchoress who calls the numbers.

"The young Welshman turned away there and muttered Salem b/witch under his breath."

He did what?


What we are told is,

"If he goes in 5v3 up, that will be a much better score than 4v4.

At 4v4, they would be all square. In that sense, this frame is crucial."


What we are told is

"The only thing permanent about technique

is that it does change."


That is the crux of it,

at the Crucible.

# MY BROTHER'S DRUTHERS

A dedication

(To my view there are two courses by which you might

run your life, as the bed knob notcher or tied to

the aproned wife. It is not for all to don one or

the other but I trust you choose well, my brother).

When you pause fumble, wait for time like on the

buses, you are jabbed and swept by its inked dry
point,

or felt tip, time honoured, a tripod refuting

passes from clacking pedestaled chalkboards; time
ladies.

When you opt to follow its token rolling churn,

you are tweeted and speckled by thrush and water
lust

and then torn away from more resistant beings

that will, only subsequently, adjourn to dust.


Cut to the leopard leap of the brave savannah:

badland danger and the purring that the planet

offers to those in despair and oleander:

a plant which fought and then rose to will.


As my brother, what part would you play?

Jazz spy, tailor, coral butcher, jailor?

The stuntman or the toiling boatman cannot

hold a glass to your lonely fervour.


We sing alone afore blackberry bushes

or die discreetly, in smart hush puppies,

discover how our follied clogging goes

when it breaks rank on lonely odd bin searches.

# Jennifer

Why trip on coral with toes in sandaled feet

and shoe the mosses of your tired retreat?


Why pawn the dowry on your downward path

then huddle up beside me, laugh?


Why come beneath me at the summer's edge

laid out so gentle, yawn and stretch?


A paintbrush to your raw emotion

scratched upon a grubby tissue.


Then tell the others of my fall;

my shoulders trembling, bones and all.

No longer will I search your skin

and you will not want for anything.

## Belvedere (Vienna)

I claim a wind to replace this roily heat
Across lawns that hold the rubbernecks' tired rap,
That it might come and roll away
The stained sweat from my baseball cap.

Young girls in pressed blouses and pants
Who save for college fall, no doubt.
Half-torn maps have given out
To aid the busy footfalls of so many tourist ants.

When they zig-zag up the sharp hill,
I stop for rest, not enduring or young
As I had been twenty minutes before
Mosquitoes pause to purr and gun.

You come back down and now we view.

And I scratch, upon pictures by Klimt and Schiele,

This boiled egg warmth and these travellers are me and you.

My time's work now is clearer.

# BEING SHONDA RHIMES

I dreamt that Derek Shepherd

was kept

in a coma

in a small flat backgammon table

in the A&E

of Seattle Grace.


Every now and then

he would shout,

"Shit Meredith, get me out of here!"

Doctor Bailey would draw close and sigh,

"I don't think he's gonna make it,

we should prepare for the worst."

Attendings nodded gravely.

Bands like Snow Patrol

did battle to place their songs

inside two precariously placed speakers,

which were hung at an angle

behind the backgammon table.


Shonda Rhimes is a TV producer,

with a capital T

and a capital V,

a Screenwriter and Author,

with a capital S

and a capital A,

and she offers creative writing courses

on the gift of narrative;

they are advertised on social media.

These courses include elements of

systematic idea generation,

dialogue and pitching,

but Derek is still in a coma

and I'm not sure

that I care.

Or that I know

why

he has been placed

in a small flat backgammon table

in the A and E

of Seattle Grace.

# TEA

Between myriad cups of tea

you and me

got well lairy

and grew up

scary.

# Tuscany in Sepia

Sting rides his scooter through a vineyard in
Tuscany.

In Italian, the past remote is rarely used.


His name is Sting,

He doesn't and he isn't; he was baptized Gordon.


T.S. Eliot used Italian sparingly in his verse—

He pronounced it ill and boomed it stilted whence
he spoke.


I live to love the present, forget T.S., Sting man and
Freddie,

I listen to Eliot now as he awaits me in my car,
downloaded ready.

Memories from when we were young are tempered in sepia,

This is now called a filter CHANGE.


We are beholden to what we read at a former time,

Moulded by the words of those who sold to us in rhyme.


Adverts were created in the post-war boom,

Americans bought fridges and stored cold foods.


When Eliot recounts his dreams, we are inspired.

When friends do it through social media, we are appalled.

# Dog on the Beach

God made me so you would have a companion.

Along the beach you tug me,

My fur is fetid and wet.

The day is dry.


Your stylish clothes trot before

Your wetted cur,

I nod and smile as you tug me

By the leash, I purr and err.


The gilthead bream sheds its oil.

The air is full of cooked sounds—

Sea cicalla, calamari

Do the rounds.

I strain to seek the smell,

The restaurant owner baulks a little.

He doesn't see I'm held by you

And my neck begins to throttle.


When I was your dog, you needed me.

I will die before you, as dogs always do.

To others I leave the signed works,

My heart will rest with you.

## Thomas 2021

Words that refer to something that does not exist
are choice:

cipher, naught,

blank, non-existence,

oblivion, nothingness,

a pink null, blackberry.


Out of nowhere,

my son told me that it was

impossible to imagine someone I'd

never seen before.


Flaming broad time ceased for three seconds,

while I considered and asked him how he knew this.

He told me he'd read it on the internet;

he's fourteen and it is 2021.


The sheep are *brebreiy*ing opposite our garden,

He now runs limber before them.


Sure enough, I gleaned, we can only process and
re-imagine

things that our brain

has several seen, places we've

already been.


We do have the ability, though, to transform

images in cholic shopping jams,

or shapes to create amalgams

on winter days or on mowed lawns.

A mirrored gate on one side reflects us in its rust,

The passing of the years, the body breathing.

I observe his graceful movement and amber reading,

in his knowing and chasing eyes I trust.

# WE HALLUCINATE OUR BOUNDARIES

In an utterance,

a sound wave of river speech,

one word runs

seamlessly

into the

next.


There are no silences

between

spoken words,

the way there are

white

spaces between the written.

When we part from each

other,

when we

inhabit

different countries,

different worlds,

all proximity is eclipsed.


You are there and,

I am here.


When you are alone and we

exchange lines,

I cannot read your calling,

though I can sense your unease and fortitude.

When you decide, you will

empty yourself into my still gentleness.

# Writing a Love Scene

I was writing a love scene and

I am not good at writing love scenes.

I was reading writers who were better than me,

far away better

at writing love scenes.

Literary and intimacy can both be chores,

their togetherness is betwixting.


"Mark," Roberta cried out, "There's a cat in the
drive. I think it's dead."

She was finely dressed, and on her way to work;

she was doubtless late.

I went outside

and there was a black and white cat in our drive

lying on its side, paws outstretched,

one eye closed, one eye open,

the one that fixed me clean.

She had come by the other day, while I was
barbequing, to say hello,

I'd naively thought (the cat, not my wife; my wife
lived with me).


"Mark," she called, "Why do they always come here
to die?"

My wife was talking about the cats.

A cat coming to die in our drive was,

in fact,

a frequent occurrence;

it happened once or twice a year.

We did not have dogs;

every other house had dogs,

and they seemed to know I would sort them out,

forego my own interests, see to their feline affairs,
their purred will,

put them to rest.


I shovelled her weight into a green bin bag and
deposited her in the tussocky wasteland

opposite where we lived.

The ants and flies had already gone to work,

her ear had been kinda' cratered, razzed at,

I patted some loamy soil over the body.


I came back into our garden.

"Mark, why are death and cats everywhere?"
Roberta asked me.

She approved of neither.

"I don't know, sweet. Go to work,

or I'll never get this love making down."

"Get it down, get it done," she said.

She was talking about the burial of the dead cat,

not my lovemaking, not my writing.


I was borrowing their ideas, the writers,

the way they curled and curved the words,

trying to capture the way they spoke of love,

although I was much better at death;

something I had always understood so much better.

# About the Author

**Mark A. Hill**'s poetry has been published in The UK Poetry Library's Top Writers of 2012 and the Live Canon 2013 Prize Anthology. He was highly commended in the 2015 Segora poetry prize and he was short-listed for the Canon 2015 First Collection Prize.

In 2016, one of his poems was commissioned, published and performed at The Victoria and Albert Museum, London, for the anniversary of Shakespeare's death: *154 New poems, by 154 contemporary poets... in response to Shakespeare's 154 sonnets.* Published in celebration of Shakespeare's 400th anniversary. His debut novel, *Mitchell Rose and The Bologna Massacre,* was published by Wallace Publishing in 2024. Highly commended in the Munster fool for poetry chapbook competition 2023. In 2024, Mark was published in DREICH and in The Pierian.

He currently resides in Cagliari, Italy where he teaches English and writes.

# PREVIOUSLY PUBLISHED

*The Crows at My Liver* (Hidden Hand, Azerate Poetry Prize Winner 2024)

*A Corpse on My Tiled Veranda* (previously published by Dreichmag, 2024)

Beauty must repeat (previously published by Live Canon Ltd. 2016)

Pasticceria Italiana (previously published by Pierian ONLINE, 2024)

Weeds in tenure (previously published by UK Poetry Library, 2012)

At the crucible (published by Southlight, 2024)

Tuscany in sepia (published by Cerasus, 2024)


Dog on the beach (published by Dreichmag, 2024)


Thomas 2021 (published by Southlight, 2024)

www.ingramcontent.com/pod-product-compliance
Lightning Source LLC
Chambersburg PA
CBHW051635120626
46551CB00014B/2084